CUCUMBERS
ARE BETTER THAN MEN BECAUSE...
PART II

Written By:
The Cucumber Group

Illustrated By:
Martin Riskin

Manufactured in the United States of America

30 29 28 27 26 25 24 23 22 21 20 19 18 17 16 15 14 13 12 11 10 9 8 7 6 5 4 3 2 1

Ivory Tower Publishing Co., Inc.
125 Walnut St., Watertown, MA 02172
Telephone #: (617) 923-1111   Fax #: (617) 923-8839

You'll never have to tell your cucumber how big it is. Cucumbers don't expect you to lie to them about their size. You never have to make a big deal over a little dill.

You'll never have to tell a soft cucumber, "Oh, it's just right. No, I don't mind. Honest, I really like it this way."

You don't have to take a 20 year medical history, get a blood test, or go to the drug store to have safe sex with a cucumber. From produce to passion, you can bag them and bed them without worrying the rest of your life.

A cucumber won't complain if you share your bed with pets, popcorn, crackers, ice cream, chocolate, magazines and romantic novels.

A cucumber won't care if you sleep with cats, dogs, or old boyfriends.

A cucumber won't be hurt
if you feel the need to lather it in KY Jelly,
love oil, or even ranch dressing.

A cucumber can get away any weekend.
You can take your cucumber on the road and it will
never insist on driving.

Cucumbers aren't afraid of flying.
Cucumbers can go as a carry-on. Even the biggest
cucumber will fit under your seat or in the
overhead compartment.

A cucumber won't complain
if you flirt with the doorman, over tip the bellboy,
or ask the young room service waiter in the tight black
pants what he's got for dessert.

A cucumber will never climax
before you do. Cucumbers never ask if you came,
if you came more than once, or if you're
like that with other vegetables.

A cucumber will never cover your walls
with stuffed fish, animal heads, or a picture of a dog
with a dead bird in its mouth.

With a cucumber, you can take your vacation whenever **you** want to go. You don't have to go to conventions and **pretend** to talk business. You'll never have to go on a sales trip and spend every hour kissing up to people you hate.

Cucumbers never expect you
to change. You won't have to get any
body parts tucked, sucked, lifted,
lowered, enlarged, reduced,
waxed or plucked for a cucumber.

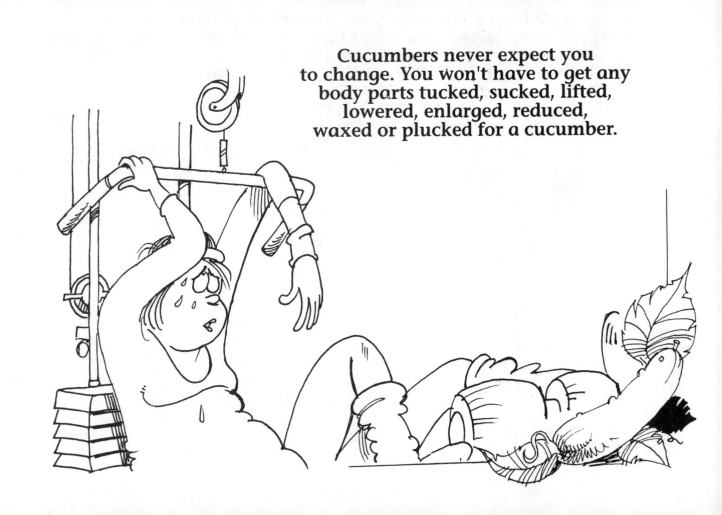

With a cucumber, you can always pick out the videos you want to see. You won't have to shop the action/adventure, sci-fi, war or horror aisle unless you want to. A cucumber will never tell you "Thelma & Louise" were butch.

Cucumbers aren't slobs.
You'll never have to pick up a cucumber's
socks, shorts, shoes, or used dental floss.

With a cucumber, the bathroom is all yours. You can leave your pantyhose, underwear and feminine hygiene products anywhere you want.

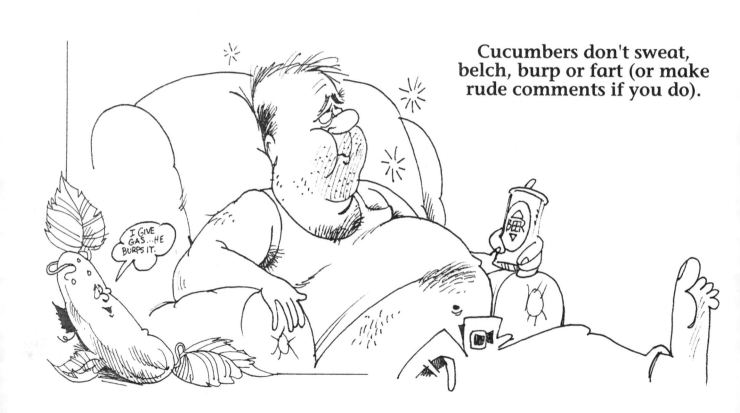

Cucumbers don't sweat, belch, burp or fart (or make rude comments if you do).

A cucumber will never ask
"How's your diet?"
at the dinner table.

Cucumbers aren't into team sports. A cucumber will never expect you to...
come to his games.
care about his games.
go into mourning when his team gets hosed.
act positively orgasmic when they win.

Cucumbers are always ready when you are.
Cucumbers don't have performance problems. You'll never
need soft music or hard liquor to get a cucumber
"in the mood."

A cucumber will never
stuff itself at a restaurant and then suggest
you split the check (you had a side salad
and diet soda.)

A cucumber will never ask you for your phone number and...

GOOD SEX LOW PRICES— IRMA

MARSHA DOES IT GOOD! 783-4176

WHY NOT MYRNA? why not? 744-8136

FOR a Good Time CALL DONNA 612-340 0372

Practice Makes PERVERTS! PERVERT HOTLINE 1-900-358 7126

Mona The Groaner 592-0163

PHYLISS 637-1139

DIVING Lessons— Call SHIRLEY 613-2149

TRY Carol— ......

write it on the bathroom wall.
give it to his friend from out of town.
give it to his teammates.
not use it.

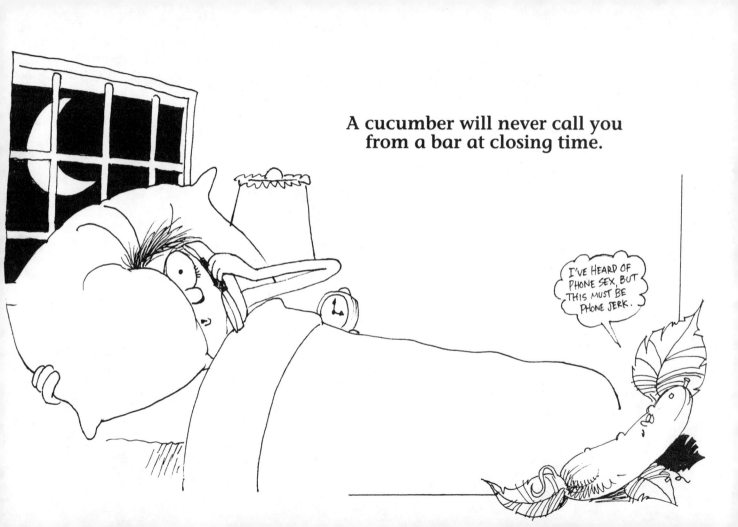

A cucumber will never
go soft in a second.

Cucumbers don't ogle other women. A cucumber will never...

subscribe to girlie magazines.
take you to the beach to study thongs.
rubberneck teenyboppers at the mall.

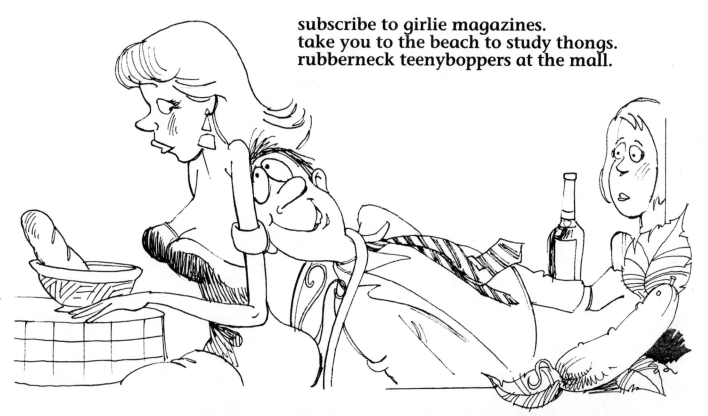

With cucumbers, you can
be any age and still get them young,
fresh and firm.

A cucumber will never wish you had

bigger	rounder	less pointed	more even
smaller	fuller	lighter	closer together
firmer	higher	heavier	further apart
softer	lower	bouncier	pointier
		jigglier	breasts.

IT'S THE NAKED TRUTH.

NUDE BATH
BEYOND THIS POIN

You'll never have to make room for a cucumber.
You can keep your closet, your drawer space, your basement,
and your garage all to yourself.

Cucumbers won't borrow your stuff.
A cucumber will never help itself to your clothes,
your car, or your credit cards.

Cucumbers come in all shapes and sizes.
Big, bigger, and hydroponic.

You'll never have to compete
with a cucumber's career, family or
hobbies for attention.

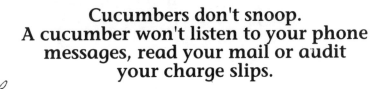

Cucumbers don't snoop.
A cucumber won't listen to your phone
messages, read your mail or audit
your charge slips.

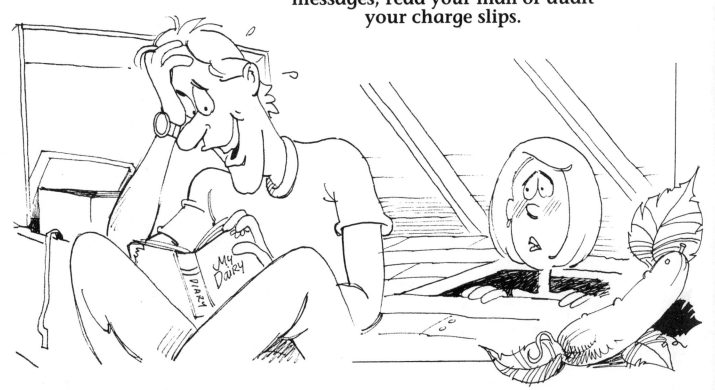

**Cucumbers don't leave town
to go hunting or fishing every time there's
yard work to be done.**

Cucumbers aren't into costumes. A cucumber will never ask you to dress like a show girl, a hooker, or a french maid.

With a cucumber, you'll never have to...
feed the team.
entertain the team.
smell the team.
clean up after the team.

Cucumbers don't need to win.
A cucumber won't be a bad sport if you're better
at sports than it is.

Cucumbers don't drink. Cucumbers don't get shitfaced, plastered, totalled, wasted or soaked. You'll never be sent home from the office Christmas party because your cucumber can't hold its liquor. A cucumber will never monopolize the party's only john while it gets sick. A cucumber will never hurl in the back of your car or on the front of your dress.

THAT'S REALLY HUGGIN' THE PORCELAIN, KID!

Cucumbers don't need flattery.
You'll never have to tell a cucumber it's the smartest, cutest,
or sexiest. You'll never have to swear it's better than all the other
cucumbers you've had before.

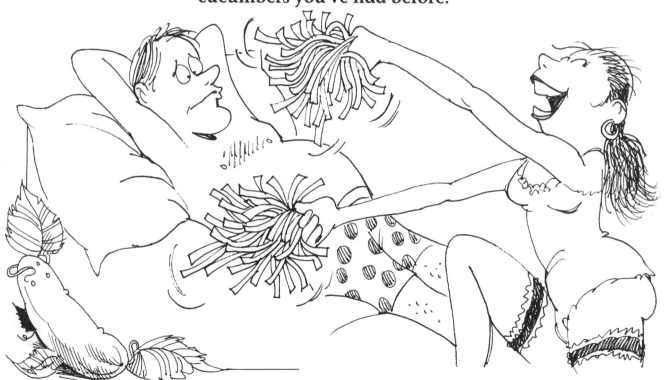

A cucumber will never tell
you how to raise the kids. Cucumbers don't expect the
kids to play baseball, basketball, and football
because they did.

A cucumber will never
want to "get it on" smelling like
smoke and beer.

A cucumber will never
eat all your food and send you
out for groceries.

Cucumbers don't have families.
You'll never have to deal with a cucumber's father, mother,
step parents, ex-wife, kids, brothers, sisters, aunts,
uncles, or cousins.

Cucumbers don't criticize your driving. A cucumber will never tell you you're too close, too fast, or too slow. Cucumbers don't get car sick and blame your driving.

A cucumber won't care if...

you can't have children.
you can't stand children.
you already have 6 children.

Cucumbers will never criticize your decorating.
A cucumber won't mind if you sleep on kitty cat sheets or bathe
with "Little Mermaid" towels.

You can spend all the holidays with your family.
At Christmas, you can open your presents
whenever you want.

A cucumber will never expect you to buy it silky boxers
or pricy sports equipment.

You don't need to feel hurt if your cucumber forgets your birthday, Valentine's Day, and anniversary.

A cucumber won't expect you to stay home from work because it gets sick.

Cucumbers will never take you for a bundle.
A cucumber won't expect you to put it through school and
dump you after graduation.

A cucumber will never tell you
you're too old, too mature, or you just
can't handle it anymore.

Cucumbers don't have disgusting eating habits. They don't play with their food, eat with their fingers, or chew with their mouths open.

Cucumbers aren't amateur athletes. A cucumber won't turn your basement into a gym, your bedroom into a locker room, or expect you to display its ribbons, awards and trophies.

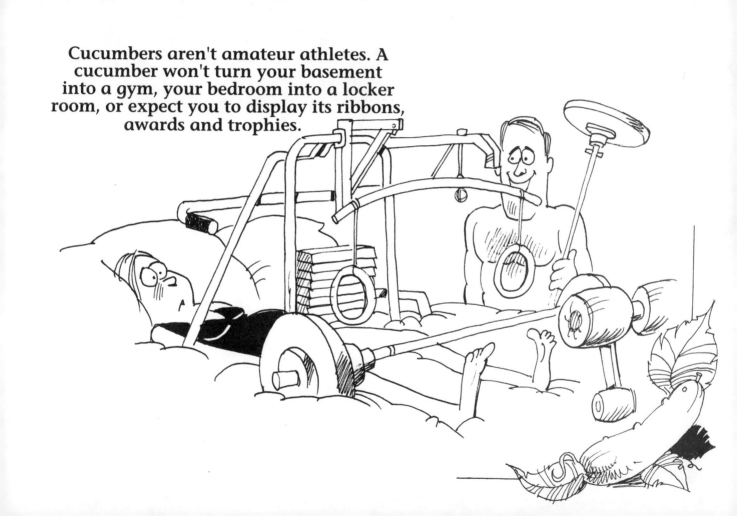

Cucumbers don't need sexual variety. They won't want to try every page in the _Joy of Sex_ or expect a different position for each day of the month.

Cucumbers don't have secretaries.
You'll never have a sneaky suspicion that the woman
at the office does more than type.

A cucumber will never tell you you're too young, too immature, or that you're just not ready to handle it.

A cucumber will never hear "yes, yes" – – when you're saying "NO, NO." You'll never have to call the cops on a cucumber.

Cucumbers never want to do it in strange places.
You won't have to fight off your cucumber in a school, church, or phone booth.

With a cucumber, you'll never have to worry about birth control. You don't need pills, jelly or foam. A cucumber will never tell you birth control is a woman's responsibility.

Cucumbers make good road buddies.
A cucumber will never sing "King of the Road" and litter your car
with sunflower seeds. A cucumber won't complain if you make it ride
in the back seat, trunk, or glove compartment.

You'll never catch your
cucumber with another woman, man, animal,
or blow up doll.

Cucumbers don't borrow stuff.

With a cucumber, you can take up the whole bed. A cucumber will never pull out the sheets, steal your blanket, or drool all over your favorite pillow.

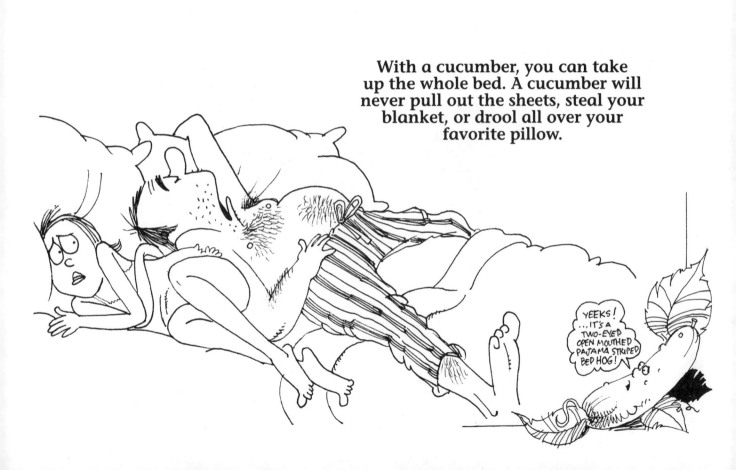

Cucumbers won't blame all your moods on
"that time of the month."

You'll never have to wrestle a cucumber for the remote control. A cucumber won't declare itself emperor of the home entertainment center. Cucumbers don't change channels, watch four sports events at once, or hit the mute switch as soon as you get interested in a show.

Cucumbers don't leave.
You'll never get a "Dear John"
letter from a cucumber.

Cucumbers don't have lawyers.
Cucumbers don't expect half
of everything.

You can always get another cucumber.

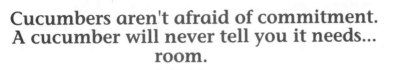

Cucumbers aren't afraid of commitment.
A cucumber will never tell you it needs...
                    room.
                    space.
                    freedom.
                    to get away for a while.

**Cucumbers don't have expensive hobbies.
Cucumbers won't criticize you for buying clothes and then drop
a bundle at the sporting goods store.**

A cucumber will never
expect you to change your name
or add a hyphen.

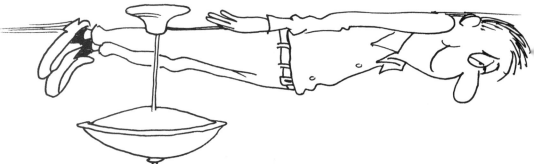

Cucumbers don't get high. Cucumbers don't snort, smoke, or shoot anything. A cucumber won't blow a lot of money trying to blow its mind.

THE MAN IS HIGH ON LIFE.

**You can dump a cucumber without feeling
rotten, cheap, guilty, or mean.**

Cucumbers don't call back or come back. You'll never have to worry about the cucumbers you left behind.

Cucumbers don't have cameras.
A cucumber will never take your picture in your bathrobe,
your bathing suit or your birthday suit.

A cucumber will never hog the paper.
You can read the funnies, clip coupons or line the cat
box with the sports page whenever you want.

Cucumbers are never
out of a job, underemployed, or going
through a career crisis.

A cucumber will never break your heart.

A cucumber will never
threaten to join the circus, a rodeo
or the Merchant Marines.

You'll never have to meet Mom.
You won't have to spend 8 hours looking through
photo albums of "my boy" or listen to stories about
that wonderful girl he <u>used</u> to date.

Cucumbers don't get jealous.
A cucumber won't cross-examine you when you stay out past nine.
A cucumber will never tell you that your "Buns" calendar is disgusting
and that the "Chip 'n Dale" dancers are all gay.

A cucumber will never borrow your car and return it smelling like a pool hall. A cucumber will never leave your car with fast food wrappers and cans in the back seat and another woman's pantyhose in the glove compartment.

Other books we publish are available at many fine stores. If you can't find them, send directly to us.

2400-How To Have Sex On Your Birthday. Finding a partner, special birthday sex positions, places to keep your birthday erection, faking the birthday orgasm, kinky sex on your birthday and much more.

2401-Is There Sex After Children? There are chapters on pre-teens and privacy, keeping toddlers out of your bedroom, great sex myths to tell your kids, how to have sex on a vacation, places to hide lingerie, where children come from, things kids bring to show and tell and more.

2402-Confessions From The Bathroom. There are things in this book that happen to all of us that none of us ever talk about. The Gas Station Dump, for example, or the Corn Niblet Dump, the Porta Pottie Dump, the Sunday Newspaper Dump to mention just a few.

2403-The Good Bonking Guide. Bonking is a great new British term for doing "you know what". Covers bonking in the dark, bonking with foreigners, bonking all night long, improving your bonking, kinky bonking and everything else you've ever wanted (or maybe didn't want) to know.

2404-Sex Slave: How To Find One, How To Be One. What it takes to be a Sex Slave, how to pick up Sex Slaves, the fine art of sexual groveling, 6 never-fail opening lines and 6 good things to know about

break-away clothing -- and more than you ever imagined.

2405-Mid-Life Sex. Mid-Life Sex is taking all night to do what you used to do all night, talking your wife into visiting a nude beach, being tolerant of farts under the covers and having biological urges dwindle to an occasional nudge.

2406-World's Sex Records. Lists the greatest sex records of all time, including the world's most success-ful personal ad, the kinkiest bedroom, the most calories burned during sex, the cheapest escort service and the greatest sex in a car -- plus many more.

2407-40 Happens. When being out of prune juice ruins your whole day, you finally fulfill your book of the month commitment, you can no longer party for 24 hours straight and you realize anyone with the energy to do it on a weeknight must be a sex maniac.

2408-30 Happens. When you no longer party all night long, you take out a lifetime membership at your health club, and you still wonder when the baby fat will finally disappear.

2409-50 Happens. When you remember when "made in Japan" meant something that didn't work, and you can't remember what you went to the top of the stairs for.

2410-Bosom Buddies. Uncovered at last--the truth about

women's bouncy parts: they're probably talking to each other! This book tells us what they would say, if only we could hear them!

2411-The Geriatric Sex Guide. It's not his mind that needs expanding, and you're in the mood now, but by the time you're naked, you won't be!

2412-Golf Shots. Humorously tells you how to look for lost balls, what excuses to use to play through first, ways to distract your opponent, and when and where a true golfer is willing to play golf.

2413-101 Ways to Improve Your Husband Or Wife. Covers how to keep your wife from losing your socks, teach your husband to clean a toilet, drive your wife crazy, and lots more.

2414-60 Happens. When your kids start to look middle-aged, when software is some kind of comfort-able underwear, and when your hearing is perfect if everyone would just stop mumbling.

2415-Birthdays Happen. When you realize your Mom may not be the greatest cook, when your biological urges dwindle to an occasional nudge, and you realize that your hairline is not receding but that your forehead is growing.

2416-The Absolutely Worst Fart Book. What is the Absolutely Worst Fart? Is it The First Date Fart, The Oh My God Don't Let Me Fart Now Fart, The Lovers' Fart, The Doctor's

Exam Room Fart? There are many choices. You choose.

2417-Women Over 30 Are Better Because... Their nightmares about exams are starting to fade, their handbags can sustain life for about a week with no outside support whatsoever, and they can eat a double hot fudge sundae and not "break out".

2418-9 Months In The Sac. A humorous look at pregnancy through the eyes of the baby, such as: why do pregnant women have to go to the bathroom as soon as they get to the store, and why does baby start doing aerobics when it's time to sleep?

2419-Cucumbers Are Better Than Men Because... Cucumbers never miss the toilet, cucumbers are always ready when you are, cucumbers won't ask "how's your diet?" at the dinner table, and cucumbers will never hear "yes, yes" when you're saying "NO, NO."

2420-Happy Anniversary: A How To Book For Husbands And Wives. This book takes all those embarrassing moments, crazy quirks, and irritating habits of your spouse, and helps you laugh at them. Learn how to deal with passion on weeknights, bathroom habits, party antics, and much, much more.

Ivory Tower Publishing Co., Inc.   125 Walnut St., Watertown, MA 02172   (617) 923-1111   **$7.00 postpaid**